Healthy Eating

for *Weight*
Management

consultant:

Lora A. Sporny, EdD, RD
Adjunct Associate Professor of Nutrition and Education
Teachers College, Columbia University

LifeMatters
an imprint of Capstone Press
Mankato, Minnesota

by
Mary
Turck

LifeMatters Books are published by Capstone Press
PO Box 669 • 151 Good Counsel Drive • Mankato, Minnesota 56002
http://www.capstone-press.com

Printed in the United States of America

Library of Congress Cataloging-in-Publication Data

Turck, Mary.
    Healthy eating for weight management / by Mary Turck.
        p.   cm. — (Nutrition and fitness)
    Includes bibliographical references and index.
    ISBN 0-7368-0709-8
    1. Nutrition—Juvenile literature. 2. Physical fitness—Juvenile literature. 3. Weight loss—Juvenile
literature. 4. Exercise—Juvenile literature. 5. Body image—Juvenile literature. [1. Weight control.
2. Physical fitness. 3. Nutrition.] I. Title. II. Series.
    RA784 .T875 2001
    613.7—dc21   00-039113
                                                        CIP

Summary: Discusses what determines healthy weight, how body image affects teens, and how to comb
diet and exercise to lose weight and to maintain a healthy weight.

Staff Credits

Rebecca Aldridge, editor; Adam Lazar, designer and illustrator; Kim Danger, photo researcher

Photo Credits

Cover: Index Stock Imagery/©Cleo Freelance
©Artville/Simiji, 11
©DigitalVision/24; Ronnie Eshel, 54
FPG International/©Elizabeth Simpson, 22
Index Stock Photos/©SW Production, 7, 29, 47; ©Mick Roessler, 17; ©Omni Photo Communications Inc., 34;
©Mark Segal, 51; ©David Davis, 52; ©Lonnie Duka, 58
Unicorn Stock Photos/©Greg Greer, 27; ©Eric R. Berndt, 37; ©Tom McCarthy, 39; ©James L. Fly, 45
Uniphoto/14
Visuals Unlimited/©Gregg Ozzo, 33; ©Jeff Greenberg, 43

A 0 9 8 7 6 5 4 3 2 1

Table of *Contents*

1 What Is Healthy Weight?   4

2 Body Image   12

3 Your Nutritional Needs   20

4 Weight Loss—Fact and Fiction   30

5 A Healthy Diet for a Healthy Body   40

6 The Importance of Exercise   48

7 Lifelong Weight Management   56

   For More Information   60

   Glossary   62

   Index   63

Chapter
Overview

- Healthy weight is a range of weights, not just one number.

- Being overweight is a problem for many adults and some teens.

- Some people use height and weight tables and body mass index to determine whether their weight is healthy.

- Good nutrition is part of maintaining a healthy weight.

- Physical activity is needed to maintain a healthy weight.

Chapter 1

What Is Healthy Weight?

Healthy bodies don't all look or weigh the same. Some people are tall and some are short. Bone structure and size are different from person to person. This variety in bone structure and size means that people have different body builds and weights.

Each person has a healthy weight range. For example, a 21-year-old woman may be 5 feet, 6 inches (1.7 meters) tall. Her healthy weight range might be 118 to 140 pounds (53.5 to 63.5 kilograms). A man may be the same age and height. He may have a somewhat higher weight range, perhaps 131 to 158 pounds (59.4 to 71.7 kilograms).

Males and females have different healthy weight ranges because their body makeup is not the same. Male bodies have more muscle tissue, and female bodies have more fat tissue. For example, breasts and the curves in the female body are mostly fat tissue. Muscle tissue weighs more than fat tissue. For this reason, a man usually weighs more than a woman of the same height.

Healthy weight is part of overall good health. Someone in good health feels well. He or she usually thinks clearly and has energy. Someone who weighs too little or too much often lacks energy and tires easily.

Overweight

About 55 percent of adults in the United States weigh too much. About 22 percent of these adults are obese, or extremely overweight. This puts them at risk for other health problems such as diabetes and high blood pressure. Diabetes is a disease in which a person has too much sugar in the blood.

Some doctors warn that obesity is an epidemic in North America. Why is this problem spreading so rapidly? Many years ago, daily life often included a lot of physical activity. Many people walked to work or school. Often, they tended gardens and swept and scrubbed floors. They usually prepared their own food, which included lots of vegetables. Many ate only three times a day.

Today, daily life has changed. Most people drive to work or ride a bus to school. They sit at a desk and work at a computer. They drive to the grocery store or pick up a meal at a fast-food restaurant. They eat constantly. Much of their food is high in fat, salt, and sugar and low in nutrition, or healthy substances. This combination of high food intake and low activity levels often leads people to become overweight.

About 20 percent of U.S. teens are overweight. These teens risk becoming overweight adults. They can avoid this risk by eating healthy foods and increasing their physical activity.

Combining a healthy, balanced diet with physical activity is the key to weight management.

Aaron, Age 14

When Aaron was in grade school, he took the bus to school every day. After school, he watched TV. Recess was the only active time of his day. When Aaron was 12, his doctor warned him that he was overweight and out of shape.

Now, Aaron bikes after school to his friend Miguel's house three days a week. He also shoots hoops with his friends on Saturdays. "I feel a lot better," Aaron says. "And I have a lot more fun. My mom used to get on my case about eating too much ice cream. Now, I eat fat-free frozen yogurt instead. More activity and my change in eating habits help me stay in shape!"

How to Measure

Measuring height and weight is easy. Telling whether someone weighs too much or too little is harder. Weight can be looked at in many ways.

Height and weight tables offer one way to look at weight. Insurance companies and doctors used to use these tables that show what weight is healthy for what height. Now, a different calculation is being used to determine whether a person is underweight or overweight. This calculation is called body mass index (BMI) and can be used for anyone older than age 2.

One pound (.5 kilograms) of fat equals 3,500 calories.

BMI is a ratio of height to weight. You can calculate your BMI by first dividing your weight (pounds or kilograms) by your height (inches or centimeters). Take that number and again divide it by your height (inches or centimeters). Then, take this number and multiply it by either 703 or 10,000. You multiply by 703 if you're using pounds and inches. You multiply by 10,000 if you're using kilograms and centimeters. Most likely, you'll have to round off your numbers as you go through the calculation. The final number you get is your BMI.

Once you calculate your BMI, you can plot the number on a BMI-for-age chart. The BMI-for-age charts are separated by ages. For children and teens, they also are separated by sex. That's because females and males grow at different rates and have different healthy weights. People of different ages, bone sizes, and body frame sizes have different healthy weights, too.

Calculate your BMI using your height and weight. On the next page, on the chart appropriate for you, locate your age on the horizontal scale. Follow a vertical line upward from your age until you reach your BMI. You'll fall on or between the wavy lines. The number at the right end of the wavy line tells you your percentile. If your BMI is below the 5th percentile, you're probably underweight. If your BMI is above the 95th percentile, you're probably overweight. A BMI above the 85th percentile but below the 95th percentile puts you at risk of becoming overweight.

Body Mass Index for Age

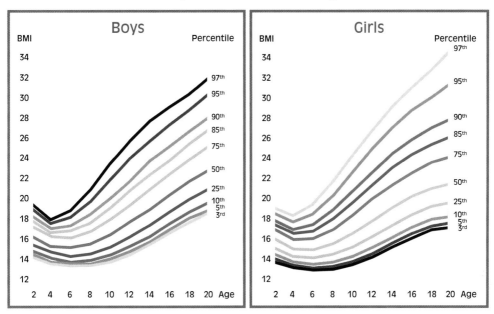

However, height and weight tables and BMI don't tell the whole story. Two people who are the same height and weight may look quite different. One may have more muscle tissue than the other. The one with more muscle tissue probably looks thinner.

Height and weight tables and BMI can help to identify people who are underweight or overweight. However, no table or calculation fits every person. The best way to determine whether you're underweight or overweight is to talk with a doctor.

Nutrition and Malnutrition

A person's diet means all the foods that the person eats. A balanced diet includes a variety of foods for good nutrition that helps a person be healthy and active.

Did You Know?

Weight can go up with TV watching. One-fourth of kids in the United States watch four or more hours of TV each day. These kids weigh more and have more body fat than kids who watch fewer than two hours of TV per day.

Many people around the world are malnourished. They don't eat enough nutritious food to maintain good health. Many times this happens because they don't have enough money to buy food.

Some scientists in North America talk about "malnutrition of affluence." Affluence, or wealth, gives people the ability to buy food. Yet, some affluent people are malnourished. This may happen because these people choose to eat too little. They may be obsessed with being thin. Their life may revolve around dieting and getting thinner. Such thought and behavior lead to malnutrition of affluence.

Poor choices also lead to malnutrition of affluence. Some people make bad choices about the food they eat. They may choose food that is high in fat and sugar and lacks vitamins and minerals needed for health. For example, these people may not consume enough calcium, which can lead to weakening of the bones.

Exercise—The Other Piece of the Puzzle

Eating puts calories into the body. These are the energy units of food that fuel the body. Most of the calories you eat are used for growth and function of body tissues. Exercise uses up calories. To maintain a healthy weight, calories eaten should equal calories burned. When people eat more calories than they use, they gain fat. When people use more calories than they eat, they lose fat. Exercise burns fat and builds muscle. As muscle increases in size, it uses more calories, even when resting.

Exercise doesn't have to be boring. It can include activities that you enjoy.

Many people think exercise is hard or boring. Samaya likes to run. Joel likes to take long walks. Both teens are involved in exercise that's good for them. Good exercise includes a variety of physical activities that you enjoy. It can include biking, swimming, hiking, and playing soccer, as well as many other activities.

Points to Consider

- Think of your daily diet—all the foods that you normally eat. What are the healthiest parts of your daily diet?

- How do you feel about using BMI?

- What is your favorite physical activity? What activities would you like to try?

- What physical activities does your average day include?

Chapter
Overview

- Because of cultural conditioning, many people think they're fat, even when they're not overweight.

- North American culture focuses on body image and weight.

- Usually, females worry more than males do about being fat.

- Genes may influence body shape and weight.

- Physical fitness is more important than weight.

Chapter 2

Body Image

Feeling Fat

Almost no one feels thin enough. Researchers talked with teen girls in British Columbia. More than 80 percent of the girls had a healthy body weight. However, fewer than 50 percent believed their weight was all right.

U.S. researchers asked high school girls if they wanted to lose weight. More than 80 percent said yes. Many of the girls were underweight, but more than half of these girls still wanted to be thinner.

Jill, Age 12

"My friends and I talk a lot about our weight. We all think we're too fat and want to be thinner.

"Luisa and I are the same height. I weigh 110 pounds, and she weighs 95 pounds. She still thinks she's too fat! She says that her stomach sticks out too much."

Marilyn Monroe was a beautiful and popular star in the 1950s and 1960s. However, by today's standards she probably would weigh too much to be a movie star.

Cultural Conditioning

Talk about body weight fills the news almost every day. TV stars tell about their weight loss. Magazines feature diet and exercise plans. Ads sell diet pills. Sometimes it may seem like almost everyone is obsessed with body fat.

In North American culture, thin often is the ideal. It's sexy and beautiful. Being overweight is undesirable. People tell fat jokes. Late-night TV shows make fun of people who are overweight. Because of what they see in the media around them, almost everyone wants to be thin.

Many teens think they are too fat and dislike the way they look. They want to lose weight. They may diet, exercise, and worry. However, most of these teens are not fat at all. The reason they have a distorted, or altered, image is because of cultural conditioning.

Imagine someone who saw the world only through television. Most people in this fictitious world would be beautiful, young, and rich. Most would be thin, too. However, the type of body that is considered beautiful changes. For example, Marilyn Monroe was one of the 20th century's most beautiful and popular movie stars. She looked gorgeous in 1960. By today's standards, she would be too heavy to be a star.

"...all the things I should have been thinking as a 13-year-old girl, adventure, what I was going to be when I grew up, my schoolwork, boys, travel, who I was...what awaited me in the world...[Instead,] I dreamt about food. My entire consciousness was taken up by food."
—Naomi Wolf, testimony to U.S. Congress

Fashion Dolls and Action Figures

Even toys encourage people to feel bad about their body. Fashion dolls are a best-selling example. Real girls cannot have doll bodies. If a fashion doll were a real female of about average height, she'd weigh 110 pounds (49.9 kilograms). She'd have a 38-inch (96.5-centimeter) chest and an 18-inch (45.7-centimeter) waist. For comparison, many women's jean sizes start at about a 26-inch or 27-inch (66-centimeter to 68.6-centimeter) waist.

In the last 30 years, action toys for boys have changed, too. Action figures have bulked up and grown enormous muscles. One particular figure had pretty normal biceps. If he were life-size, those front arm muscles would measure 11½ inches (29.2 centimeters)—about average for an adult male. The new figure has biceps that would be 26 inches (66 centimeters). That's bigger than any body builder in history has had!

Real Bodies, Real People

Many people want superstar good looks. They think dolls are pretty and action figures are handsome. They want to be like the models in fashion magazines. They may dislike the way their own body looks.

Real people don't look like toys or supermodels. Actors and models look different from the rest of us. Before 1980, the average fashion model weighed only 8 percent less than the average woman. In 1999, the average fashion model weighed 23 percent less than the average woman. Some supermodels starve themselves to stay thin for the camera.

When people starve themselves to stay skinny, they miss out on vital nutrients. Fashion dolls and action figures don't need to think about these substances in food needed for good health. Their plastic body will last forever. However, real people need to take care of their body. They need nutrition and activity to maintain a healthy weight.

Bodies Around the World

In the real world, people come in all shapes and sizes. In many parts of the world, plump is beautiful. Having a big body may show that a person is rich enough to eat well. People who weigh more may have higher social status than those who weigh less. Skinny girls may be thought of as unattractive and poor, while heavier girls appear beautiful and shapely.

However, TV shows spread North American culture to other parts of the world. For example, until recently in the Fiji Islands, people found big women beautiful. They liked the look of large and muscular women and men.

In 1995, TV arrived in the Fiji Islands, and people began watching North American shows. After TV arrived, researchers saw changes. Suddenly, girls began talking about diets. By 1998, three out of four Fiji girls said they felt too big or fat. Some admitted vomiting, or throwing up, to try to lose weight.

Until North American television shows appeared in the Fiji Islands, heavy women were considered more attractive than thin women were.

Body Fat and Gender

More females than males worry about being fat. First, North American culture often values women based on how young and thin they look. Second, female bodies store fat differently than male bodies do. As children, both boys and girls have low body fat—about 8 percent. A girl's body fat increases at puberty, when a child's body changes to an adult's. During that time, a girl's body fat goes up to about 22 percent.

Having body fat is part of being female. Females need more body fat than males do because their body is prepared to have babies. If body fat drops too low, so does the hormone estrogen. A hormone controls specific body functions. If a female's estrogen level is too low, her body won't function as it should. Menstruation may stop. This is a female's monthly loss of blood and tissue. Low body fat and estrogen also can cause difficulty in bearing children and can weaken bones.

The male body is shaped differently. Boys gain muscle mass instead of fat at puberty. Their body doesn't need the same fat distribution that a female's body does. For example, boys usually develop broader shoulders, while girls develop wider hips.

What Shapes Your Body?

No one gets fat just from eating too much. Body weight and shape depend on three things. First, your food intake sets the amount of energy you consume. Second, your body composition, growth rate, and activity level determine how much energy you use. Finally, your genes help determine your body type. Genes control specific characteristics in a living being. You get your genes from your parents. Food intake, body composition, growth, activity level, and genes work together to determine weight and shape.

People are overweight for different reasons. Sometimes overeating causes people to weigh too much. More often, lack of activity causes people to become overweight. Some people's genes make them likely to be overweight.

Glen, Age 17

"All my life, I've been the biggest kid in my grade. I was teased a lot about being fat. Then I went out for wrestling. My coach explained that I had a large body frame. I'd never be skinny, but I could get fit. So I began to work out.

"I still weigh more than the tables say I should. I probably always will. My doctor said it runs in my family. Both my parents are heavy, too. But now I'm fit. I can run a mile and I use weights. I'm strong, and I finally feel good about my body."

Anyone Can Be Fit

Like Glen, people of all body types can be fit. They can have a body that feels good and works well. They can be both strong and flexible. To achieve and maintain fitness, healthy eating and physical activity are essential.

Points to Consider

- What jokes or talk have you heard about body size? How do such comments make you feel?

- What body types do you see in your family?

- Which is more important to you—being fit or being thin? Why?

Chapter
Overview

- Food provides fuel for body maintenance, growth, and activity.

- Food guides can help you choose a balanced diet.

- Different foods contain different nutrients, such as carbohydrates, proteins, and fats.

- Teens have special nutritional needs.

- Fiber and water are essential parts of a healthy diet.

Chapter 3

Your Nutritional Needs

Fueling Your Body

Food provides fuel for the body and brain. The body needs fuel, just as engines need fuel. All engines need the right kind of fuel to run well. Nutritious foods provide the right fuel for our bodies. Human bodies slow down when they run out of fuel. People lack energy. They still move, but not as fast. They may feel tired or grouchy. The brain slows down, too.

Vang, Age 17

"Every day, I need a snack after school before wrestling practice. I usually eat a piece of fruit and a sandwich. That gets me through practice.

"One day, I forgot to bring a snack. I had really low energy. My moves were sluggish. Pete almost pinned me. I wrestle better than Pete does, but that day I wasn't feeling strong. Ask any athlete. We eat right to stay strong and in shape."

The Food Guide Pyramid can help you choose the right balance of foods to eat daily.

Choosing Nutritious Foods

People need to eat a variety of foods for good nutrition. Different foods contain various nutrients. The body needs many kinds of nutrients to work well. Research has shown which nutrients your body needs and how much. Both the U.S. Food Guide Pyramid and Canadian Food Guide to Healthy Eating show results of that research. The Canadian guide looks like a rainbow. You can use these guides to help choose foods for good nutrition.

The pyramid and rainbow show what kinds of food the body needs and in what quantities. They show that you need more plant foods than animal foods. For example, you need more fruits and vegetables than dairy products.

Within each food category, you have many choices. Within the bread/grains group, you can choose pasta, bagels, tortillas, rice, and breakfast cereal. It's up to you to decide which of these foods to eat. The following chart shows the number of servings from each food group recommended for active teens.

Food labels show a recommended percentage of daily values (percent DV) based on a daily diet of 2,000 calories. The percent DV tells you how much of the recommended daily amount one serving of the food contains.

Recommended Daily Servings for Active Teens

	Serving for boys	Serving for girls
• Bread/grains	11	9
• Vegetables	5	4
• Fruits	4	3
• Milk foods	3 to 4	3 to 4
• Meat and meat substitutes	3	2
• Fats, oils, sweets	Very little	Very little

Fuel for Activity and Growth

Teens need energy to do work and to fuel growth. Carbohydrates, proteins, and fats provide this energy. Active teens need about 2,200 to 3,000 calories per day. Adults need energy from food for work, but not for growth. Most adults need about 2,000 calories each day.

The body uses vitamins in small quantities. These tiny amounts are necessary for specific body functions.

Carbohydrates

Starches and sugars are both carbohydrates. Rice, potatoes, cereals, and breads are some examples of foods that contain starches. They provide calories as well as other nutrients. For example, potatoes provide fiber, vitamin C, and potassium. Fiber is a part of food that the body doesn't digest. Fiber helps foods move through the digestive system. Potassium is a mineral that helps the body maintain its fluid balance.

Sugars include sweeteners such as white sugar, molasses, honey, corn syrup, and maple syrup. All sweeteners but one contain calories but no other nutrients. Dark, or blackstrap, molasses is the exception. This sweetener contains both calcium and iron. Because of their lack of nutrients, almost all high-sugar foods are called empty calories. Besides sweeteners and the foods made with them, fruits and milk are naturally rich in sugar. More than half of a person's daily calories should come from carbohydrates.

Proteins

Proteins not only provide energy but also help build and repair body tissues. Good sources of protein include low-fat or nonfat milk, eggs, meat, poultry, fish, and beans. About 15 percent of a person's daily calories should come from proteins.

Fast Fact

Fats

Everyone needs to have some fat in his or her diet. The body needs fat to build nerve cells and produce hormones. Fat helps to absorb and store some vitamins in the body. Fat also provides fuel. Less than 30 percent of daily calories should come from fats in foods.

Gram for gram, fats have even more calories than sugar. The body needs only about one tablespoon (15 grams) of fat daily. The average American eats six to eight tablespoons (90 to 120 grams) a day. Excess fat in food can be stored easily within fat cells in the body.

Vitamins and Minerals

Vitamins and minerals don't provide calories for energy. Instead, the body uses very small amounts of vitamins and minerals for specific functions. For example, vitamin A helps maintain healthy skin and eyesight. Fruits and vegetables provide many essential vitamins, including vitamins A, C, and several of the B vitamins.

Vitamin and Food Supplements

Some people take vitamins, minerals, or other food supplements. These provide doses of nutrients in pill or liquid form. They may help supply nutrients that are missing from the diet. Supplements must be used with caution. Taking a daily multivitamin and mineral supplement with 100 percent of the daily value (DV) for most nutrients is safe. Taking higher doses of vitamins or minerals can be harmful. Therefore, it's best to talk with a doctor before taking any high-dose supplements.

It's better to get vitamins and minerals through foods rather than supplements. That's because foods contain many other nutrients and healthful nonnutrient substances as well. For example, drinking milk is better than taking calcium pills. Eating oranges is better than taking vitamin C tablets.

Teen Nutritional Needs

Teens have different nutritional needs than adults or children do. This is because teens are growing rapidly. During puberty, a teen may grow an inch or a couple centimeters in a month or two. Some teens noticeably gain weight for the first time. Active teens need to eat more healthy food during these years to support this growth.

Teens need more calcium and phosphorus than most adults do. These minerals help support bone growth. About half of adult bone mass is developed during adolescence. Therefore, teens need about 1,300 milligrams of calcium and 1,250 milligrams of phosphorus daily. Teens need to get vitamin D because it helps the body absorb calcium and phosphorus. Most teens do not get enough calcium in their diet. However, phosphorus intake by teens is usually more than ample.

Milk products, tofu, and navy beans are good sources of calcium. Meat, poultry, fish, eggs, beans, whole grains, and nuts are good sources of phosphorus. Milk and fish provide vitamin D.

Teens also need more iron than most adults do. Girls need more iron as they begin menstruation. Boys need more iron as they build muscle. Teens need 12 to 15 milligrams of iron daily.

Iron comes from red meats and liver, egg yolks, poultry, and fish. Some dark green, leafy vegetables, such as spinach, contain iron. Other foods are fortified with iron. That means iron has been added to them. Food labels can tell you whether a food contains iron.

Foods with fiber promote a healthy digestive system.

Fiber and Water

Fiber, a structural part of plants, and water are the dynamic duo essential for healthy digestion. Yet most Americans eat only half the recommended 20 to 35 grams of fiber daily.

Fiber moves through the stomach and small intestines without being digested. It holds onto large amounts of water. The combination of fiber and water prevents two problems. Fiber and water prevent constipation, which makes it hard for the body to rid itself of solid waste. The two also prevent diarrhea, a condition in which normally solid waste is runny and frequent. Vegetables, fruits, beans, and whole grains are good sources of fiber. Because most fiber-rich foods are filling, they may help people eat less and lose weight.

Water regulates body temperature, carries nutrients and oxygen to cells, and cushions your joints. Water is essential for almost every body function. The average person loses 10 cups or about 2.5 liters of water daily. This is done during urination when the body rids itself of liquid waste. It's also done during breathing and perspiration, or sweating. Some water is replaced by water contained in the foods we eat. However, about 8 cups (1.9 liters) must be replaced daily by drinking fluids.

Most teens don't eat enough fiber. There is a way to figure out the daily grams of fiber that you need to eat. Take your age and add five. For example, a 13-year-old should eat at least 18 grams of fiber daily.

Most liquids help fill your daily water needs. The exceptions are liquids containing caffeine and alcohol. These liquids actually dehydrate, or take water out of, your body. So, if you drink coffee or soda, you probably need to drink more water to make up for it!

Pa Lia, Age 14

"I like to drink fruit juice. By comparing the labels, I can tell which kind of juice is healthier for me to drink. One brand has 38 grams of sugar per serving and only 10 percent of the recommended daily value (DV) of vitamin C. Another brand has 100 percent of the DV for vitamin C and only 21 grams of sugar. I choose the second!

"I know my body needs lots of calcium. At my age, I need more than the DV on the label. I don't like to drink milk. So I look for calcium in other foods. I like yogurt, and that has as much calcium as milk. I also choose an orange juice brand that is calcium-enriched. Extra calcium is added to this orange juice. Each serving has 35 percent of the DV for calcium."

You choose the foods you eat. You can make nutritious choices and share your good health with friends.

Making Your Own Choices

You choose the foods you eat. Like Pa Lia, you can select foods with the nutrients you need and make healthy food choices. Learn about your nutritional needs. Read food labels on prepared foods. Learn which foods contain which nutrients. Make good choices for your own health.

Points to Consider

- Which nutrients do you think are most often missing from your daily diet?

- What are your favorite foods? Which nutrients do they contain?

- How do your eating habits measure up against the food pyramid or rainbow?

- Do you read food labels? Why or why not? How can they be helpful?

Chapter
Overview

- Rapid weight loss diets of any kind almost never work in the long run.

- Fad diets usually do not provide good nutrition and the weight loss that results rarely lasts.

- Many diets aren't good for teens because teens need enough calories and nutrients for proper growth.

- Some people try weight loss pills, products, and programs. Many of these diet techniques can be harmful.

- People need to make lifestyle changes to lose weight and maintain that weight loss. These changes include eating a more healthy diet and getting plenty of activity daily.

Chapter 4

Weight Loss— Fact and Fiction

People try all kinds of diets. Lori followed a cabbage soup diet that a friend told her about. Nate cut out salt and cut down on everything else. He was following the advice of his wrestling coach. Cassandra tried a high-protein, low-carbohydrate diet that she found in a magazine. Vang counted calories. Keisha fasted, or didn't eat, for two days.

All of them lost weight, and all of them gained it back. Each of them thought the diet worked and felt bad about gaining back weight. For most people, dieting is like a yo-yo, because their weight goes up and down. When their weight goes up, they diet and lose weight. Then they regain weight and look for a new diet. The new diet "works" for a while, and they lose some weight. Usually, they gain it back again.

Fad Diets

Fad diets are popular weight loss plans. However, they often provide poor nutrition because of limited food choices. The weight loss they deliver rarely lasts. Most fad diets depend on water loss for quick results. Sooner or later, the body regains the lost water weight.

The high-protein, low-carbohydrate diet Cassandra tried is one example of a fad diet. This diet puts excess ketones in the blood. These are chemicals the body makes when carbohydrates are in short supply. The extra ketones upset the body's chemical balance. The body tries to get rid of the ketones by ridding itself of fluids. Thus, weight loss!

Dieting Health Risks for Teens

Fad diets aren't good for adults or teens. But even diets that are safe for adults may not be safe for teens. That's because a low-calorie diet doesn't provide enough calories and nutrients teens need for growth. This can have long-term consequences. One of the most important effects is that bones may be weakened permanently.

Brandi, Age 16

"I started dieting when I was 12. The first diet I tried was a high-protein diet. Some doctor wrote a book about it, so I thought it must be good. I cut out carbohydrates and ate only meat and salads for two weeks. I lost 9 pounds! Then I went back to regular eating, and I gained the weight back.

"Now that I'm older, I know more about dieting. I don't do fad diets like the protein thing any more. I just count calories. I watch the scale. If I put on 2 pounds, I go on a low-calorie diet until I lose the weight. I still have to diet about once a month."

Dieting can be like a yo-yo because body weight continues to go up and down.

The Diet Yo-Yo

Brandi may no longer be doing fad diets, but she is still on the diet yo-yo. Why does the weight keep coming back?

Low-calorie diets change the body's metabolism. This is the rate at which the body uses food for growth and energy. A low-calorie diet tricks the body into "thinking" it's starving, so the body's metabolism slows down. A slower metabolism burns fewer calories.

After the diet, Brandi returns to normal eating, but her metabolism remains slow. Her body uses less food for energy and packs away the rest as stored fat, so she gains weight again.

Anorexia nervosa is an emotional problem that needs treatment.

Beyond Diets—Eating Disorders

Ginny, Age 15

"Michelle is my best friend. She's really skinny, but she always wants to lose weight. She never eats French fries, pizza, or burgers. She eats absolutely nothing with added sugar! She only eats vegetables and fruits, and not really much of them. Her usual lunch is a handful of lettuce with no dressing. She counts every single calorie. She's 5 feet 3 inches tall, and she weighs only 85 pounds. I'm worried about her."

Michelle may have an eating disorder called anorexia nervosa, or just anorexia. People with anorexia try to control their body by not eating. They also may use extreme exercise to establish control. Lack of food causes malnutrition and damage to body organs, especially the heart and kidneys. In its final stages, anorexia may cause death.

"I had one 16-year-old patient who dropped to 74 pounds and was hospitalized. She couldn't understand why she was in the hospital because she said she was eating a balanced diet. Well, her diet was balanced, but there wasn't enough of it. She was eating only 600 to 700 calories a day but needed 1,700 to 2,000."
—Dr. Alexander R. Lucas, from the Mayo Clinic, talking about one patient with anorexia nervosa

Bulimia is another eating disorder. It's sometimes called bingeing and purging. People with bulimia eat a large amount of food, especially high-calorie food. Then, they usually make themselves vomit. Some people with bulimia use laxatives or exercise obsessively. Laxatives are drugs that loosen solid body waste and help its release happen quickly. Like anorexia, bulimia is a dangerous attempt to control one's body.

Both of these disorders are emotional problems that require treatment. If you or someone you know has symptoms of an eating disorder, you can get help. Talk with a parent, doctor, teacher, nurse, or school counselor. Some resources about eating disorders are listed at the back of this book.

Pills, Potions, and Programs

People try many different approaches to losing weight. Some try diet pills or drugs that can cause heart damage, high blood pressure, dehydration, and malnutrition. Some of these diet drugs may be habit-forming, causing a kind of drug dependency.

Other people may try diet drinks or diet foods. These often are expensive. If tied to exercise plans, they may work for some people. However, in the long run, diet drinks and diet foods cannot take the place of healthy eating habits.

Some people use diet gadgets that can be dangerous, too. One popular gadget is a rubber suit that's supposed to help the body sweat off weight. The only weight lost is water weight. The suit is dangerous because it can raise body temperature to harmful levels.

Many people try weight loss programs that claim success. Ads for these programs may say things such as, "Take weight off—and keep it off!" Often, the ads are dishonest; they are created to sell, not to inform. Some programs promise a magic combination of foods that helps your body burn fat. These usually aren't based on scientific proof. They also may be unhealthy.

The best way to lose weight is to increase physical activity and change eating habits.

Limited Successes in Dieting

Some diet programs do show limited success. Often, these are long-term diet programs that include exercise. Many people enjoy the support of others at weight-loss center meetings. For them, such a plan may work. Other people may not like paying for meetings. Some may not want to monitor their food constantly. For them, such a plan doesn't work well.

Studies show that few people lose weight and keep it off by dieting, no matter what plan they use. Only 5 to 10 percent of dieters keep weight off for a year.

Losing Weight Without Dieting

So, how do people manage to lose weight and keep it off? They lose weight when they burn more calories than they consume. Healthy weight loss takes time. Lifestyle changes offer the best way to lose weight. Most people need to eat differently and become more active.

Noua, Age 13

"I was a real couch potato. Every day after school, I watched TV and snacked on cookies, chips, or sugary cereal.

"Then I decided to change my lifestyle. I decided to get 30 minutes of exercise almost every day. And I decided to change most of my afternoon snacks to fruit and unbuttered popcorn. On Fridays, I would treat myself to a couple of cookies or a small bag of chips.

"I started taking my dog for a walk after school. He loved it! After a few weeks, I did, too.

"I didn't lose weight right away. In fact, the scale didn't show any weight loss for three weeks. But even after the first week, my clothes fit a little better, and I felt more energetic.

"I have lost a little weight. My body shape has changed a lot. But best of all, I love the way I feel."

Becoming more active can include playing football with friends or even walking the dog.

Healthy eating provides nutrients you need with the calories you use. It cuts empty calories. For example, soda pop has calories but no real nutritional value. If you mix orange juice with sparkling water instead, you get fewer calories and lots of nutrition.

Using more energy means becoming more active. You don't have to run miles or do hundreds of jumping jacks. That kind of exercise can be boring! Walking your dog, swimming, playing soccer, even cleaning house all are ways to use more energy. Staying active is the key to losing weight and keeping it off.

Points to Consider

- What fad diets have you heard about? Do you think they would work well? Why or why not?

- Have you ever gone on a diet? What did you do and how did you feel?

- What are the good and bad features of going on a diet?

- What are some ways you could add more physical activity to your daily routine?

Chapter *Overview*

- The first steps in eating for weight management include listening to your body and discovering your eating habits.

- Nutritious breakfasts and nutritious snacks are part of a healthy eating plan.

- No foods are forbidden foods.

- Be careful of portion sizes—you may be eating more than you think you are.

Chapter 5

A Healthy Diet for a Healthy Body

Listening to Your Body

Our body can tell us when we need to eat. Hunger is the body's signal that it needs food. The body can lose this natural ability and send confused signals about when, what, and how much to eat.

How does the body get confused? Dieting is one way. When people diet, they don't pay attention to hunger. They only pay attention to the diet plan. Advertising can confuse natural hunger signals, too. Ads can make people want to eat. Their brain ignores natural hunger signals. Instead, these people respond to advertising images and messages.

People can relearn their body's natural signals. Before they eat, they can think about whether they really are hungry. They can eat slowly. This gives the stomach time to realize that food has arrived and then signal the brain. When people pay attention to their body's signals, it can help them to eat in a more healthy way.

Improving Eating Habits

Many people don't pay attention to what they eat. Because they're in a hurry, they may go through the day eating snacks or meals that are convenient.

Jeremy, Age 15

"My mother told me I should stop eating so many sweets. I didn't think I ate many sweets. I thought I ate pretty healthy foods, so I decided to prove that Mom was wrong."

Jeremy started keeping an eating journal. Every time he ate something, he wrote it down in a little notebook he kept in his pocket. At the end of the week, Jeremy showed the journal to his mom.

Jeremy says, "We were both surprised. I was right about sweets. I ate ice cream almost every day, but never candy or cookies. However, I hardly ate any fruits or vegetables. The only fruit on my list was orange juice. I knew I had to make some changes."

Jeremy took the first step toward healthy eating. He discovered what he was eating by keeping track of what he ate for a whole week. Then he looked at his eating patterns. Jeremy found that his diet needed to change to be healthy.

Some 20 to 24 percent of teens skip breakfast. Skipping breakfast means starting the day without enough energy. Often, teens who skip breakfast don't do as well in school as teens who do eat breakfast.

You may think you know your eating habits. Perhaps you do. The best way to find out is to keep a record. Write down everything you eat for a week. Then you can decide whether you need to make changes.

Getting a Healthy Start

Healthy eating starts with a healthy breakfast. This is the most important meal of the day because the body has been without food for so long. It's possible that the body hasn't had food for 10 hours or more. So it needs to refuel in the morning. A healthy breakfast should provide one-fourth to one-third of the day's calories and nutrition.

Healthy doesn't have to mean boring. Jacki likes to have a breakfast shake. She makes the shake with 8 ounces (240 milliliters) of fat-free milk. She adds a cup (225 grams) of frozen strawberries and a tablespoon (15 grams) of chocolate syrup. Along with the shake, she eats a slice of whole-wheat toast. She starts her day with servings of milk, fruit, and grains from the pyramid and rainbow guides.

Byron prefers to start his day with a slice of ham in an English muffin. He drinks a glass of fat-free milk every morning, too. His day begins with servings of meat, grains, and milk.

Macy likes black beans. Many mornings she has black beans in a tortilla and a glass of orange juice. She starts her day with servings of meat substitute, grains, and fruit.

Dried fruit is a good snack. One-quarter cup (60 grams) of raisins has 100 calories and contains fiber and iron. One-quarter cup (60 grams) of dried apricots has 110 calories and contains vitamin A and potassium.

If it's not swimming in butter and salt, popcorn is a healthy snack choice. It has lots of fiber.

Each breakfast could be even better. Jacki could eat her toast with peanut butter. That would add a serving from the meat group to her breakfast. Byron could add a piece of fruit to his breakfast. If Macy added low-fat cheese to her tortilla, she'd have a milk serving. Even without these changes, the breakfasts are healthy. Healthy doesn't mean perfect. Healthy means a balance of nutritious food eaten throughout the day.

Healthy Meals and Healthy Snacks

Breakfast is the most important meal of the day, but lunch and the evening meal are important, too. The body needs to refuel regularly. Healthy choices at lunch and dinner make up important parts of a healthy diet.

Snacks also offer good opportunities for healthy eating. Sarah likes to eat fresh fruit for a snack. Sam prefers a glass of fat-free milk and graham crackers. Nick enjoys low-fat cheese and whole-grain crackers. Nora eats raisin bran with fat-free milk. Each has chosen a healthy snack.

Choosing snacks can be tricky. Most energy bars say they're packed with nutrition. Often, they also are packed with sugar and salt. Too much sugar or salt is unhealthy. Sugar is a high-calorie ingredient that offers no other nutrition. Too much salt can cause high blood pressure and weakened bones.

Healthy eating doesn't mean giving up your favorite foods such as brownies. It just means eating them only once in a while.

Fruit juice and low-fat or fat-free milk are healthy drink choices. But watch it! The word *fruit* on the label doesn't guarantee nutrition in the can or bottle. Some "juice" products contain lots of added sugar with little real nutrition. Check the food label and ingredient list to know what you're getting. How much sugar is in a serving? How many servings are in a can or bottle? Which vitamins does the drink contain?

No Forbidden Foods

No foods are forbidden. Let's say you love chocolate. Healthy eating doesn't mean you have to give it up entirely. You can eat chocolate. You just need to keep it in its place and take charge of your cravings. First, you can try to ride out the urge. When you want to grab a chocolate bar, wait. Find something else to do for 15 minutes. After a short time has passed, check in. Do you still want chocolate?

Second, start small. Eat 25 chocolate chips instead of a whole bag. Measure out your chocolate treat and then sit and savor it slowly. Finally, take it easy on yourself. Splurging, or indulging, now and then is okay. If you're eating healthy foods every day, a little splurge won't hurt, so you don't have to feel guilty.

Changes in your life can affect your eating habits. Such changes might include getting an afterschool job, hanging out with new friends, and dating.

Watching Portion Size

Jarrad, Age 15

Jarrad went to a restaurant with his sister and grandparents last night. He ordered his favorite food—a plate of spaghetti topped with two large meatballs. "Great nutrition choice," Jarrad thought to himself. "I've got a serving of vegetables in the tomato sauce, pasta for a serving or two from the grain group, and a serving of meat."

Let's take a closer look at Jarrad's meal. Like many restaurants, the one Jarrad went to knows that its customers like to see a full plate. The cook starts the spaghetti plate with a full 3 cups (675 grams) of pasta. That's equal to six servings of grains! More than a cup (225 grams) of tomato sauce covers the spaghetti for two healthy servings of vegetables. Each of the large meatballs is equal to one serving of meat. Two of them are almost enough meat for the whole day. That's a lot of servings at once!

If Jarrad didn't want such a large dinner, he could take half of his meal home. Then he'd have only three servings of grains and one serving of meat at dinner. He could have the rest for lunch the next day. Or, he could have asked for an extra plate and split the dinner with his sister.

One step toward a healthier diet is keeping a food diary to keep track of your eating habits.

Portion size is important for a healthy diet. One slice of bread or a half cup (115 grams) of cooked rice, pasta, or cereal is a single grain serving. One-fourth of a bagel or one-half of an English muffin is a single serving. A large bakery muffin may be three or four grain servings and usually has lots of fat and added sugar.

Making Good Choices

The following are three steps toward a healthier diet:

1. Get an accurate picture of what you eat. Keep a food diary for a week. Write down what, when, and how much you eat.

2. Make healthy food choices, starting with a nutritious breakfast. Choose a variety of foods for good nutrition and watch portion sizes.

3. Think about what you eat but don't get down on yourself. Everybody splurges now and then. What matters is the progress you make toward a healthy, everyday diet.

Points to Consider

-   How reliable do you think your body's hunger signals are?

-   Which food groups do you need to eat from more often? How could you do this?

-   If you could change two things about your eating habits, what would they be? How could you work toward making these changes?

Chapter
Overview

- Exercise helps to control weight and has other health benefits.

- Stretching exercises make a good beginning.

- Aerobic exercises are good for the heart and lungs.

- Weight training improves strength and builds muscle.

- Some people feel they're too busy for exercise. They don't have to do 30 minutes of exercise all at once. They can split it into three 10-minute sessions throughout the day.

Chapter 6

The Importance of Exercise

Exercise

Exercise is the second part of the weight management solution. Exercise revs up the metabolism, so the body uses more food energy. Exercise tells the body to burn fat to fuel the muscles.

Say the word *exercise* out loud. Does it bring to mind activity that is boring and difficult? Now say the word *play*. That seems different! People like to play because it's fun. Swimming, biking, and playing volleyball all are play activities. They also are good exercise.

Few people want to look ahead to boring, difficult exercise every day for the rest of their life. The key to staying physically active is finding fun activities. Those activities are different for each person.

Begin stretching by reaching for the sky. Reach first with one hand and then the other. Stand on tiptoes as you reach. Then bend down, fingertips toward the floor. Remember that you're stretching, not straining, so your stretch shouldn't be painful.

Ashley, Age 13

"I don't like to exercise alone, and gym class is boring. A few kids in my class are real jocks, and they look good. I'm not too good at the games we play. I always feel like everybody's watching me.

"I tried playing soccer in a summer league when I was 10. I liked the game, but I didn't like the league. All the other kids had been playing since they were in kindergarten. I felt out of place.

"But now, some of my school friends and I play soccer after school, just for fun. We laugh a lot and get great exercise. It's okay if somebody screws up. We're not playing to get the most points; we're playing to have a good time."

Ashley may not be too good at soccer, but soccer still can be good for Ashley. Even if she doesn't play well, the activity helps her to burn calories and build muscle.

Move for Good Health

Nearly half of all teens don't regularly engage in vigorous physical activity. Often, older teens are even less active than younger teens. Girls usually are less active than boys are.

Being physically active benefits a person in many ways, including reducing feelings of depression and anxiety.

Regular physical activity improves health in many ways. Regular exercise reduces risks of heart disease, high blood pressure, and diabetes. It reduces feelings of depression and anxiety. Exercise helps build healthy bones, muscles, and joints.

Any physical activity that burns calories and builds muscle is exercise. Dancing is an example of great exercise. Playing fetch with a dog is better exercise than watching TV.

Mixing It Up for Fitness

Combining three kinds of exercise improves physical fitness. Stretching improves flexibility and prevents injury. Aerobic exercises help heart and lung health. Weight training exercises improve strength, posture, balance, and coordination while increasing muscle mass.

Stretching

It's important to stretch before exercising. However, your muscles should be warm before you stretch. If you're going to jog, walk first for at least five minutes and then stretch. At the end of an exercise session, stretch again. Doing some slow stretches gives muscles a chance to cool down gradually.

Aerobic activity works your heart and lungs.

Exercise Target: Heart and Lungs

Doctors recommend at least 30 minutes of aerobic exercise three or more times a week. Aerobic activity is vigorous exercise that increases the heart rate and the amount of oxygen taken in. Some examples of aerobic exercise are jogging, biking, swimming, jumping rope, and in-line skating.

You can measure how vigorous your activity is by taking your pulse, or heart rate. Count the number of heartbeats in 15 seconds and multiply by 4. That's how fast your heart is beating per minute. For example, say you count 28 beats in 15 seconds. Multiply 28 times 4. That equals 112 beats per minute.

If you're working hard enough for aerobic activity, your heart rate should be in your target heart rate range. To determine this range, you first find your maximum heart rate. You can do this by subtracting your age from 220. However, this isn't your goal.

The target heart rate range for beginners is 50 to 75 percent of the maximum heart rate. People in good shape can exercise harder. Their target heart rate might be as high as 85 percent of their maximum heart rate.

Target heart rate ranges for teens

At a Glance

Age	50 to 75 percent	85 percent
17	102 to 152	173
16	102 to 153	173
15	103 to 154	174
14	103 to 155	175
13	104 to 155	176
12	104 to 156	177

Tania, Age 15

Tania loves playing basketball on her school's team, the Cougars. During basketball season, she practices for at least an hour every day. During the off-season, she runs to keep in shape.

"When I started running, I started out slowly," Tania explains. "Gradually, I built up both speed and endurance. I check my heart rate to make sure I'm pushing myself hard enough for good exercise."

To find her target heart rate range, Tania first subtracts 15 from 220. This is her maximum heart rate, which equals 205 beats per minute. Her target heart rate range is 75 to 80 percent of 205. So she multiplies 205 by .75. That equals 154. Then, she multiplies 205 by .80, which equals 164. Tania's target heart rate range is 154 to 164 beats per minute.

Weight training improves muscle tone and increases strength and muscle mass. This is important because muscle burns more calories at rest than fat does.

Weight Training for Muscle Power and More

Training with weights builds muscles. Weight training is sometimes called a static exercise because it's not aerobic. Weight training should be combined with aerobics for a complete exercise program.

A weight training program can reshape and tone your body. A physical education teacher, sports coach, or trainer at a health club may be able to help you. He or she may be able to give you advice on the right weight training program for you.

Weight training can be complicated or simple. Different movements work and build different muscles. Some people use machines. Other people use free weights, or dumbbells. Others even may use 1-pound cans of vegetables or heavier milk cartons for weights.

Taking Time, Making Time

Zoe, Age 17

"I know you should have 30 minutes of vigorous physical activity several times a week. But I just don't have the time. I get on the bus early in the morning. After school, I have a job. After supper, I have homework. I don't have 30 minutes anywhere in my day. I can't get sweaty before school or my job. So the only possible time to exercise would be at night. By then, I'm too tired."

You can do some easy things to add physical activity throughout your day:

- Walk up stairs instead of taking the elevator.

- Take a short walk around the block.

- Take an activity break; get up and stretch or walk around.

Did You Know?

Zoe needs to know some exercise solutions. First, she doesn't need to exercise for 30 minutes in a row. She'd get almost as much good out of three 10-minute sessions in a day. She doesn't have 30 minutes in the morning, but she probably has 10.

Second, she doesn't need to sweat to get the benefits of exercise. Sure, a heavy workout is good for you. But moderate activity helps, too. A 10-minute walk would help a lot. Third, exercise will add to her energy. If she takes time for exercise, she will feel better. By homework time, she may not be so tired.

Exercising longer, harder, or more often is great. The more exercise you get, the greater the health benefits. However, moderate exercise helps a lot, too. So take several short exercise breaks during the day. Any exercise is better than none!

Points to Consider

- What are some fun activities that also are good exercise?

- Create an exercise program for one month. What activities does it include? How do each of these activities help your body and health?

- How do you or could you fit 30 minutes of exercise into your day at least three times a week?

- How many minutes of physical activity do you get each day? Do you think this is enough? Explain.

Chapter
Overview

- Feeling good about your body is part of a healthy lifestyle.

- Weight management is important to both teens and adults.

- A healthy lifestyle includes good choices about food and activity.

Chapter 7

Lifelong Weight Management

Making the Most of Your Body

Liking your body is part of liking yourself. If you like yourself, you're on the road to having good mental health and living a happy life. Some people find it difficult to like their body. They look in the mirror and see only problems. They always want to look like someone else. If you want to like your body, you have to get real. You need to appreciate the body you have and let go of unrealistic goals.

Like Martin, you can make healthy choices for yourself, including choosing nutritious foods and getting lots of exercise.

Sonia, Age 14

Sonia's mom and dad are both overweight. Her father has heart problems because of his weight.

Sonia wants to be healthy. She bikes, swims, and stays active. She eats healthy foods. She wears size 12 jeans. She's not skinny, but she's not fat either.

Sonia looks muscular and fit. She has many friends. Sometimes she thinks she'd like to be skinny. She knows that isn't realistic for her. Most of the time, she likes how she looks.

Lifelong Weight Management

Weight management remains important throughout life. Most people gain weight as they get older. Most people also lose muscle mass and strength as they age because they stop exercising. The loss of muscle mass causes the body to use fewer calories throughout the day. The same healthy habits that help teens manage weight can help them as adults, too.

Weight management is all about healthy choices. Each person chooses what, when, and how much to eat. Each person chooses whether to be active or a couch potato. You can make your own healthy choices for your best possible future.

Just being skinny isn't the same as being healthy. Everyone needs to choose foods for good nutrition. Everyone needs exercise to build strength and endurance.

Did You Know?

Martin, Age 19

"I graduated from high school last year and I live on my own. I juggle college, work, and everything else.

"Now I'm responsible for my own health. My mom isn't fixing meals for me. She doesn't tell me to wear a hat when it's cold. I make my own choices now.

"I want to make healthy choices. I try to keep fruit and low-fat yogurt in the refrigerator. I avoid fast food. I try to eat a healthy breakfast every morning. I bring granola bars, bananas, and multigrain crackers to work. That way I can eat healthy snacks when I'm hungry, instead of chips from the vending machine.

"I love to walk, and that helps a lot! I walk to bus stops or the grocery store. I walk everywhere I can. I probably walk 4 miles a day. I feel great, and I've never looked better."

Points to Consider

- When you look in the mirror, what do you like best? Why?

- Do you think that making healthy choices as a teen is easy or hard? Explain.

- What are three choices you can make for a healthy future?

Note

At publication, all resources listed here were accurate and appropriate to the topics covered in this book. Addresses and phone numbers may change. When visiting Internet sites and links, use good judgment. Remember, never give personal information over the Internet.

Internet Sites

Health Canada: Canada's Food Guide to Healthy Eating
www.hc-sc.gc.ca/hppb/nutrition/pube/foodguid/foodguide.html
Contains nutrition information recommended by Canadian health experts

The Healthy Refrigerator
www.healthyfridge.org
Contains information and recipes for heart-healthy eating and general nutrition for children and teens

KidsHealth.org for Teens: Food and Fitness
http://kidshealth.org/teen/nutrition
Provides information on nutrition, dieting, exercise, and sports

Mayo Health Clinic
www.mayohealth.org
Provides thorough online health information on a variety of topics, with special sections on nutrition and weight management

Nutrition on the Web for Teens
http://library.thinkquest.org/10991/teen12.html
Has many articles about nutrition by teens and for teens; also includes myths, case files, and recipes.

Something Fishy Website on Eating Disorders
www.somethingfishy.org
Provides information and chat on eating disorders

Useful Addresses

American Dietetic Association (ADA)
216 West Jackson Boulevard
Chicago, IL 60606-6995
1-800-877-1600
1-800-366-1655
www.eatright.org

Health Canada
Health Promotions and Programs Branch
Nutrition and Healthy Eating Program
Jeanne Nance Building, Tunney's Pasture
Ottawa, ON K1A 1B4
CANADA
www.hc-sc.gc.ca

United States Department of Agriculture
(USDA)
Center for Nutrition Policy and Promotion
(CNPP)
Office of Public Information
1120 20th Street Northwest
Suite 200, North Lobby
Washington, DC 20036-3406
www.usda.gov/cnpp

For Further Reading

Gedatus, Gus. *Exercise for Weight Management.* Mankato, MN: Capstone, 2001.

Gregson, Susan R. *Healthy Eating.* Mankato, MN: Capstone, 2000.

McCoy, Kathy, and Charles Wibbelsman. *The Teenage Body Book.* Rev. ed. New York: Perigee, 1999.

Nissenberg, Sandra K., and Heather Nissenberg. *I Made It Myself!: Mud Cups, Pizza Puffs, and Over 100 Other Fun and Healthy Recipes for Kids to Make.* Minneapolis: Chronimed Publishing, 1998.

Turck, Mary. *Healthy Snack and Fast-Food Choices.* Mankato, MN: Capstone, 2001.

Glossary

aerobic (air-OH-bik)—requiring oxygen, air; energetic exercise that strengthens the heart.

anorexia nervosa (an-uh-REK-see-uh nur-VOH-suh)—an eating disorder in which people don't eat enough to be healthy

bulimia (buh-LEEM-ee-uh)—an eating disorder in which people overeat and then force their body to rid itself of the food

calorie (KAL-uh-ree)—a measurement of the amount of energy that a food supplies

carbohydrate (kar-boh-HYE-drate)—a nutrient that provides energy; sugars and starches are carbohydrates.

fad diet (FAD DYE-uht)—popular eating plan for losing weight; fad diets rarely provide long-lasting weight loss.

fat (FAT)—a nutrient that provides energy and is stored in the body

gene (JEEN)—a code within cells that determines specific characteristics and functions in a living being

heredity (huh-RED-uh-tee)—passing along certain traits from parents to children through genes

malnutrition (mal-noo-TRISH-uhn)—a harmful condition caused by not eating enough food or by eating the wrong kinds of food

metabolism (muh-TAB-uh-liz-uhm)—the process by which the body turns food into energy

nourishment (NUR-ish-muhnt)—food substances necessary to maintain life

nutrient (NOO-tree-uhnt)—a substance necessary to stay strong and healthy

obesity (oh-BEE-suh-tee)—the condition of being more than 20 percent over healthy weight

Index

action figures, 15–16
anorexia nervosa, 34, 35. *See also* bulimia

blood pressure, high, 6, 35, 44, 51
body composition, 5, 18
body fat. *See* fat tissue
body image, 13–19, 57
body mass index (BMI), 7–9
bones, 5, 8, 26
    weakening of, 10, 17
bread/grains, 22, 23, 27, 43, 46–47
breakfast, 43–44, 59
bulimia, 16, 35. *See also* anorexia nervosa

calcium, 10, 24, 26, 28
calories, 10, 23, 24, 25, 39, 43, 44, 50, 51, 58
    counting, 32, 34
Canadian Food Guide to Healthy Eating, 22
carbohydrates, 23, 24
cultural conditioning, 14, 16, 17

dairy products, 22, 23, 59. *See also* milk
dehydration, 28, 35
diabetes, 6, 51
diet, 6–7, 9, 18, 21, 41–47. *See also* portion sizes
    and improving eating habits, 7, 42–43
    pills, drinks, foods, and gadgets, 14, 35–36
    and your nutritional needs, 21–29

dieting, 10, 14, 31, 41
    fad, 31–32
    and health risks for teens, 32
    limited successes in, 37
    losing weight without, 37–39
    low-calorie, 32, 33
    yo-yo, 31, 32, 33
dolls, fashion, 15–16

eating disorders, 34–35
emotional problems, 10, 16, 34–35, 51
energy, 6, 18, 23, 25, 33, 38, 39, 49, 55
estrogen, 17
exercise, 6, 10–11, 14, 35, 37, 49–55
    aerobic, 51, 52
    extreme, 34, 35
    increasing, 7, 37–39
    through sports, 21, 49, 50, 52, 53, 58
    time for, 54–55
    weight-training, 51, 54

fat, 6, 10, 14. *See also* fat tissue
    feeling, 13–15
    stored, 17, 33
fat tissue, 5, 9, 10, 14
    and gender, 17
fats, oils, sweets, 23, 25, 42, 44, 45
females, 5, 8, 15, 17
fiber, 24, 27, 28, 44
fit, feeling, 6, 18, 19, 38, 58
food labels, 23, 26, 28, 29
fruits, 22, 23, 24, 25, 26, 27, 28, 42, 43, 44, 45, 59

genes, 8, 18
growth rate, 18

Index

heart, 34, 35, 51, 52, 58
height, measuring, 7–9

iron, 24, 26, 44

journals, 42–43, 47
juice, 28, 45

lifestyle choices, 7, 29, 37–39, 42–43, 46, 47, 58, 59
lungs, 51, 52

males, 5, 8, 15, 17
malnutrition, 9–10, 15–16, 34, 35
meat and meat substitutes, 23, 26, 43, 46. *See also* proteins
media, 14, 15, 36, 41
menstruation, 17, 26
metabolism, 33, 49
milk, 24, 26, 43, 44, 45. *See also* dairy products
minerals, 10, 25–26
muscle tissue, 5, 9, 58
muscles, building, 10, 17, 26, 50, 51, 54

nutrients, 22, 25–26, 29, 32, 39
nutrition, 6, 9, 16, 39, 43
  needs for good, 21–29
  needs for teen, 26

phosphorus, 26
physical activity. *See* exercise
portion sizes, 46–47
potassium, 24, 44

proteins, 23, 24. *See also* meat and meat substitutes
puberty, 17, 26

rubber suit, 36

salt, 6, 31, 44
size, 5, 8, 16, 18, 58
snacks, 21, 38, 44, 59
splurging, 45, 47
starches, 24
stretching, 50, 51
sugar, 6, 10, 24, 25, 44, 45
supplements, food, 25–26

target heart rate, 52, 53
television, 7, 10, 14, 16, 17

U.S. Food Guide Pyramid, 22

vegetables, 6, 22, 23, 25, 26, 27, 42, 44, 46
vitamins, 10, 25–26, 44, 45
vomiting, 16, 35

water, 27, 28, 31, 36
weight. *See also* body image
  healthy, 5–11, 16, 18
  loss, 31–39
  management, 57–59
  measuring, 7–9
  over-, 6, 7, 9, 14, 18, 58
  regaining, 31, 33
  under, 9–10, 13, 15
  wanting to lose, 10, 16, 13, 34–35